Sounds

by Diana Kimpton

Contents

Sounds all around	2
Making sound	4
Speaking and singing	6
Hearing sound	8
Helping ears to hear	10
Echoes	12
Thunder and lightning	14
Glossary/Index	16

Sounds all around

Sounds are all around us.
Some sounds are loud.
You can hear them easily.
Some sounds are quiet.
You have to listen carefully
to hear them.

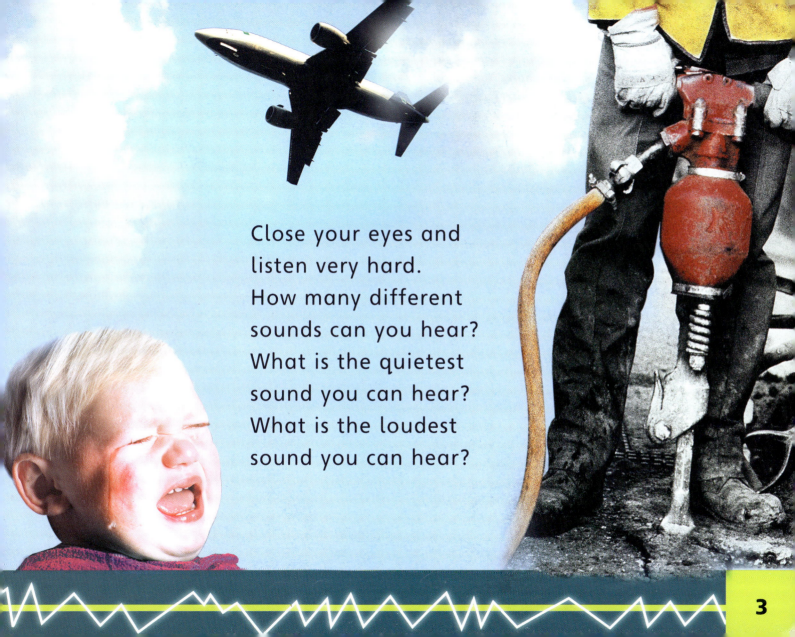

Close your eyes and listen very hard. How many different sounds can you hear? What is the quietest sound you can hear? What is the loudest sound you can hear?

Making sound

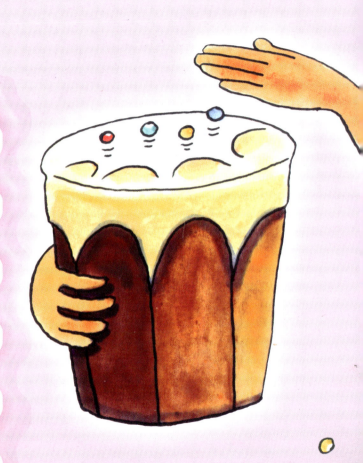

When you hit a drum, the top of it moves up and down very quickly. It makes a sound. You can see the movements if you put tiny beads on the top of the drum. This kind of movement is called a **vibration**.

When you pluck a rubber band on a box guitar, the rubber band moves backwards and forwards very quickly. It makes a sound. When the top of the box and the rubber band move, they make the air move too.

These movements in the air are vibrations. The vibrations in the air are the sound.

A box guitar is made of a tissue box, rubber bands, and a pencil.

Speaking and singing

When we speak or sing, we make movements in the air.
You can feel the movement if you hold your hand in front of your mouth.

Put your fingers on the middle of your throat and hum. Can you feel a shaking movement with your fingers? This movement is a vibration.
It makes the sound by making the air vibrate.

Try making some different sounds. Feel how the vibration changes.

You can change the sound by changing the shape of your mouth or by moving your tongue. Your mouth and tongue change the way the air is moving. This changes the sound.

Hearing sound

Sound travels through the air to your ears.

The part of your ear you can see is called your outer ear. It helps the sound go into the hole in your ear. This hole leads to the inner ear, which you can't see.

hole leading to inner ear

The sound goes through the hole to your **eardrum**.
Movements in the air make the eardrum move.
The eardrum makes some tiny bones move.
This movement goes to the inner ear.
The sound is sent from the inner ear to the brain.

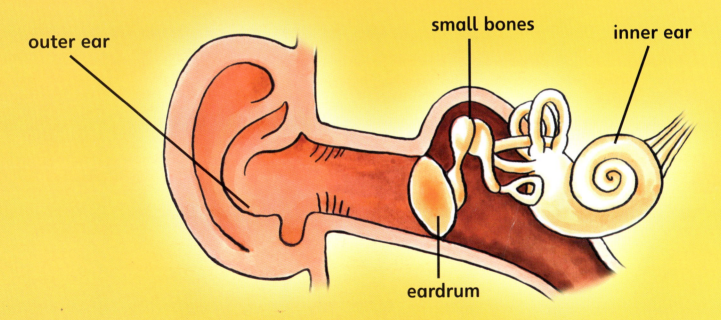

Helping ears to hear

Your heart makes a sound but it is very quiet. The doctor uses a **stethoscope** to help him hear it.

Some people find it hard to hear sounds. They use a hearing aid to make the sounds louder.

Road workers often need ear protectors.

Some sounds are so loud that they can hurt your ears. People who work near loud sounds wear ear protectors. These stop loud sounds from reaching their ears.

Echoes

When you shout, the sound spreads out in all directions. If the sound hits something solid, it bounces off it like a rubber ball bouncing off a wall. The sound that bounces back is called an **echo**.

- echo
- sound
- solid wall

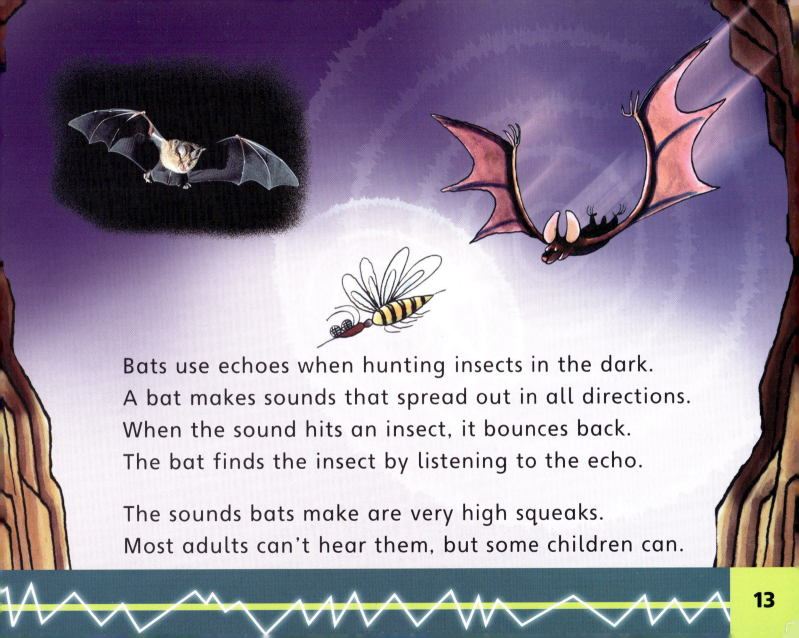

Bats use echoes when hunting insects in the dark.
A bat makes sounds that spread out in all directions.
When the sound hits an insect, it bounces back.
The bat finds the insect by listening to the echo.

The sounds bats make are very high squeaks.
Most adults can't hear them, but some children can.

Thunder and lightning

Thunder is the sound made by **lightning**. If you are standing very close to lightning, the sound is very loud. You see the lightning and hear the thunder at the same time.

If the storm is further away, you see lightning first and hear thunder later.
This is because sound travels more slowly than light. The light reaches your eyes before the sound reaches your ears.

As the storm moves away from you, the time between the lightning and the thunder gets bigger.
The thunder sounds quieter too.

Glossary

eardrum	a piece of skin in the inner ear
echo	a repeat of a sound which bounces off a hard surface
lightning	a flash of light in the sky caused by electricity in clouds
stethoscope	an instrument used by doctors for listening to the heart
vibration	a rapid movement to and fro

Index

drum	4	lightning	14-15
ear	8-9, 9-10	outer ear	8-9
eardrum	9	singing	6
ear protectors	11	speaking	6-7
echo	12-13	stethoscope	10
hearing aid	10	thunder	14-15
inner ear	8-9	vibration	4-5, 6-7